BANGKOK

IAN LLOYD

WILLIAM WARREN

TIMES EDITIONS

Bangkok
Times Editions
422 Thomson Road, Singapore 1129

First published 1986
© Copyright 1986 Times Editions
All rights reserved for all countries

Designed by Viscom Design Associates
Printed by Tien Wah Press, Singapore
Color separation by Colourscan, Singapore
Typesetting by Superskill, Singapore

ISBN: 9971-40-024-3

CONTENTS

The Intricate Mosaic

World on the Water

A Spiritual Spectrum

Beauty Sacred and Profane

Sanuk Diversions

Eternal Bangkok

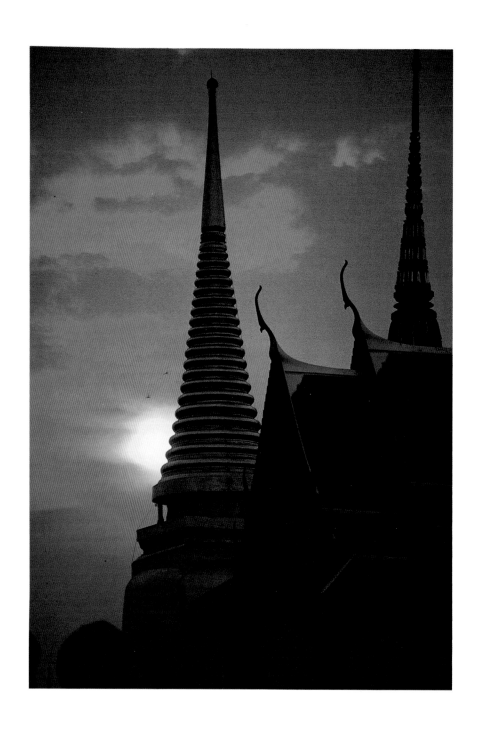

The Intricate Mosaic

"And who can describe a city as to give a significant picture of it? It is a different place to everyone who lives in it."

Thus wrote Somerset Maugham, circa 1929, expressing not only a general truth but also a specific frustration. Maugham was in Bangkok for the first time and, like countless others before and after, he was having trouble getting a firm imaginative grip on what he called "this strange, flat, confused city".

Maugham was coming down with a nearly fatal case of malaria, contracted in northern Burma, and his literary perceptions may have been a trifle jaded. Later, when he felt better, he did manage to work up a considerable degree of enthusiasm for Bangkok's dazzling Buddhist temples and for its exotic waterways. Yet the difficulties he encountered with the city as a whole, never fully resolved, are echoed by numerous Western visitors today.

Whatever their preconceptions of the place — "the Venice of the East", a gigantic set for *The King and I*, an unabashed Babylon of varied vices, just a reasonably comprehensible metropolis — the complex reality bewilders and sometimes appals them. It is not only vast (covering some 1,500 square kilometers) but apparently without coherent plan; many of its streets appear on no existing maps, even though they are lined with drab, already weatherstained rowshops. The noise is of a decibel level undreamed of in Maugham's day, the heat still terrific for much of the year, the traffic horrendous even by the high standards of most Asian cities: all of which inhibits adventurous forays very far off the beaten tourist track. "Why do people want to live here?" some of these visitors ask plaintively, before they depart for a more orderly, rational place like Singapore.

(The question, it might be noted, is nothing new. "When I rose on my first morning in Bangkok and took a glance at things around me," wrote an American missionary in 1835, "I could scarcely resist the sense of foreboding that assailed me. Oh how different, I thought, from what it was in Singapore. How gloomy the dwellings of the missionaries here when compared with the charming house we had occupied on that attractive island.")

Well, why *do* people live in Bangkok, both *farangs* like myself and some six million Thais (nobody really knows exactly how many)? The answers, as Maugham suggested, are necessarily varied, often conflicting, sometimes mysterious. Mine, I'm sure, would be different from those of the retired civil servant who lives next door, from the Chinese banker who lives behind me, from the widowed aristocrat who lives across the road; and their motives, their perceptions of the city, would differ from one another's. We perhaps complain about the same things — the traffic and the periodic floods, the noise and the pollution, the potholes in the street and failings of the police — but we would probably find little in common if we sat down together to analyze its charms.

I felt more kinship with a fellow *farang* who once told me his reason for taking up residence. Somehow, long before he actually came, a copy of the *Bangkok Post* found its way to the California town where he lived, and perusing it he came upon an intriguing news report. A tram car in the city, it seemed, had hit a pedicab, which in turn had rammed into a taxi, causing the vehicle to swerve and fall into a canal on top of a boat selling charcoal, "I knew then and there," he said, "that I just had to live in a place where such things could happen."

For me, too, much of Bangkok's appeal, ever since I arrived 25 years ago, has stemmed from the serendipitous surprises that seem to lie around every corner, in such profusion that I have never come close to developing a complacent attitude.

Out for an evening stroll, I discover a pleasant new garden restaurant calling itself the Bangkok Snake House, which proves indeed to specialize in various reptiles, slaughtered live at tableside (fresh cobra blood, the owner promises me, is a surefire aphrodisiac). Caught in a traffic jam, I find myself gazing up a flight of gleaming marble steps, on which are arrayed, as if especially for my private pleasure, a brass band in red-and-gold uniforms, a Chinese lion dance troupe, and a file of solemn, saffron-robed Buddhist monks (all, it transpires, taking part in the opening of a new office building). On a routine visit to a friend in hospital, I take a wrong turn and wander into a museum of forensic medicine, where the chief exhibit is a famous murderer, embalmed and stark naked (he ate the livers of his victims, a group of schoolboys inform me with delighted shudders). Pruning shrubs in my garden one morning, I look up to find an elephant gravely regarding me from over the wall (the mahout was charging five *baht* to walk under the animal, an experience believed to bring good fortune).

None of my neighbors would have taken much delight in these experiences or, for that matter, have looked on them as being all that extraordinary; "Oh him," was the widowed aristocrat's reaction when I told her about the pickled murderer. Nor would the loquacious taxi driver who takes me to work in the morning, the polite students whom I teach at the university, the diminutive literature professor who shares my office (though she wrote her Ph.D. thesis on Tennessee Williams), the sidewalk vendor who sells me a chunk of chilled pineapple between classes. They see different aspects of the city, some of which are still as strange to me as to a visitor who stepped off a plane last night.

To all of them, it is important to remember — indeed, to all Thais — Bangkok is as much symbol as city: not merely 45 times bigger than Chiang Mai, its nearest contender, but also the source of power and the center of just about everything materially and intellectually desirable. The monarchy, probably the single most unifying force in Thai society, is based in Bangkok, although members of the royal family spend a good deal of the year on provincial tours. So is the Supreme Patriarch of Thai Buddhism, all the ministers who run the government, the most powerful military commanders, and the heads of nearly all the leading business firms and financial institutions.

Bangkok has the country's top schools, colleges, and universities; until the late 1960's it had the *only* universities, and though now there are several provincial ones, a place at prestigious Chulalongkorn or Thammasart University remains the dream of every ambitious high school graduate. It has the best medical facilities, both public and private. It has huge, air-conditioned shopping centers (five new ones opened in a single month toward the end of 1984), department stores, luxury hotels, massage parlors, laser-lit discos, roller-skating rinks — in brief, bright lights. Above all, it has jobs, and with them the ever-alluring promise of social and economic ascent.

One of the most popular Thai movie plots concerns the country boy who forsakes his village to seek his fortune in Bangkok; and the lower echelons of the city's society are primarily composed of people who have done just that. Get into any taxi or *tuk-tuk* (motorized tricycles) and nine times out of ten the driver will be an immigrant from the chronically poor north-east. The family land has been lost, or the crops have failed, or perhaps it was merely those beckoning bright lights; and so here he is, coping with the city's fearsome traffic — making it *more* fearsome, in the opinion of some, since he has a decidedly fatalistic attitude toward the lethal potential of the motor vehicle.

Country girls come, too, for the same reasons; they find work as domestics, as seamstresses in one of the many garment factories, as members of construction crews (where they work every bit as hard as the men), as waitresses, go-go dancers, masseuses, or (if they are lucky) as a "minor wife" of some wealthy merchant.

Though their stay may extend to a lifetime, few of these immigrants ever think of Bangkok as truly "home". They are thus in a different category from the Chinese who could claim, with some justice, to be the city's oldest real residents. In 1782, when King Rama I decided to move his capital across the river from Dhonburi, a thriving Chinese community was already on the site of his proposed palace. He moved them a mile or so downstream to a district that soon became the commercial center and that is still today the most clearly identifiable "Chinese" area.

Along its clamorous, traffic-clogged streets thousands of businesses, some of them operating from a single room, deal in everything from gold to outboard engines, from baby chickens to hand-carved coffins (ordered in advance). Signs as often as not are in Chinese, and so are the snatches of conversation you hear above the din; dropped down unawares, you could easily imagine yourself in one of the older districts of Hong Kong or Singapore.

The impression would be misleading in more ways than one, however. Through intermarriage at all levels, plus a little prodding from the government (all citizens, for example, must have Thai names to qualify for official documents), the Chinese have been so thoroughly assimilated, in both outward appearance and inner loyalties, that practically no one can distinguish them, or bothers to try. "My father and mother were Chinese," a student once told me, "but I am Thai." And so she was, in everything that mattered.

Also in another category are the numerous employees of the government, which requires 40 closely-printed pages of the local telephone directory to list all its ministries, departments, and organizations. Both powerful and obscure, these range up and down the gamut of Bangkok society: lowly clerks perpetually shifting papers in cavernous, Kafkaesque offices, traffic policemen under the glaring sun, university lecturers explaining the subtleties of Shakespeare, doctors and nurses at public hospitals, drivers of over-crowded city buses, beribboned military officers at parades, black-gowned judges in courts of law, important-looking officials getting out of limousines at the vaguely Arabian Nights confection that serves as the Prime Minister's office.

All these — and others, too: Buddhist monks and Indian merchants, society ladies and street vendors, assorted *farangs* and members of the old aristocracy — form parts of the intricate mosaic of Bangkok life. And like the pieces of a mosaic, however variously shaped, they find themselves co-existing in remarkably close proximity, for as even the most casual visitor perceives, this is no orderly city of carefully-zoned neighborhoods.

You will find the humblest of sidewalk restaurants, specializing in spicy north-eastern food and patronized principally by homesick *tuk-tuk* drivers, just outside the walls of a palatial mansion done up in the quasi-French decor known locally by the all-embracing name of "Louis"; a squalid slum of insubstantial shanties and rickety boardwalks not far from a lavish massage parlor with one-way mirrors that allow a customer to discreetly select the girl of his choice; a movie theater adorned with lurid, three-storey billboards half concealing a quaint old Victorian bungalow, all gingerbread fretwork and generous verandahs that once over-looked cool gardens; a serene Buddhist *wat* of classic Thai architecture surrounded by the most mundane modern rowshops.

Would-be town planners (and there are some in Bangkok) naturally deplore such a hodgepodge and regularly issue dire warnings of impending civic breakdown. Others like myself prefer what someone has called "the pleasures of chaos", finding in Bangkok's unexpected juxtapositions an essential part of its appeal. However long I make it my home I will never claim to know all, or perhaps even most, of its many lives; nor do I want to, for variety and a dash of puzzlement are other components of its flavor.

Giving further vent to the frustration he felt in Bangkok and similar "populous modern cities of the East", Maugham suspected "that they have after all something to give you which, had you stayed longer or under other conditions you would have been capable of receiving. For it is useless to offer a gift to him who cannot stretch out a hand to take it".

I wouldn't presume to speak for all the others, but the gift Bangkok offers me is an assurance that I will never be bored.

Bangkok is a river city. In the chaos of its modern streets this is sometimes easy to
forget, but the great Chao Phya still dominates the older areas where
the capital began its sprawl into surrounding rice fields. Here the porcelain- encrusted
Temple of Dawn rises on the west bank, while in the distance can be seen
the spires and multi-tiered roofs of the Grand Palace.

Hundreds of Buddhist temples, both celebrated and obscure, are scattered
throughout greater Bangkok, offering tranquil refuge from the city clamor just
outside their walls. Overleaf, monks stroll serenely through the grounds
of one, carrying ceremonial fans to be used in one of the countless rites in which
clergy play a vital part, from funerals to the blessing of a new office building.

Thailand's royal family plays a highly visible role in the national life, officiating at countless ceremonies as well as undertaking arduous provincial tours to inspect various projects. Left, one of the royal limousines arrives at the Grand Palace for a ritual at the adjoining Emerald Buddha Temple. King Bhumibol Adulyadej and Queen Sirikit are shown above in the temple precincts, greeting reverent subjects who gather for every public appearance.

The Thai sense of sanuk or "fun" is a pervasive part of Bangkok life, as is the famous Thai smile, which can illuminate even the most solemn occasions. The students on the left are not, as it may at first appear, registering mass displeasure at a boring lecture but rather demonstrating support for a football team, while the beaming young men above are doormen at a luxury hotel.

Mythological creatures stand guard at Wat Phra Keo, home of the Emerald Buddha, above. For much of Bangkok's history the highest point in the flat city was the Golden Mount, right — Phu Khao Thong to Thais.

Several streets in Bangkok's older section are devoted almost entirely to shops
selling assorted images and furnishings for Buddhist temples. The one
on the left displays massive gilded bells and Buddha images, while the
figures above include some holy ascetics. Such items are generally presented
by groups or individuals as a way of making merit and frequently
have the donor's name inscribed on them.

Overleaf, members of the Royal Guard in traditional uniforms march past one of
the old European-style buildings in the palace compound. The carpet across
the courtyard has been specially laid for the King who, though shorn today
of absolute powers, is still revered by Thais of all classes.

Military uniforms have always been a part of the Bangkok scene. The figures above, carved on the doors of a temple, display both a traditional Thai outfit and one inspired by 19th century Europe. Contemporary soldiers, right, in less exotic attire stand outside the Temple of the Emerald Buddha.

Overleaf, during one nervous period following the collapse of Indo-China, a popular joke proclaimed Bangkok to be safe from invasion: the enemy would certainly be stopped dead at the outskirts by the city's horrendous traffic. Numerous solutions, from flyovers to one-way streets, have been attempted, without much noticeable success.

Everything looks right except the price tag. Despite complaints from foreign manufacturers — and threats by the Thai government — artful imitations of Western luxury items continue to attract delighted buyers like the happy tourist on the right. His enthusiasm may be somewhat tempered, however, after his discovery comes back from the first washing.

Despite their resemblance to Thailand's famous temples, the elegant little structures above have nothing to do with Buddhism. They are the future homes of the spirits who guard almost every house and commercial building, placated daily with various offerings. The girl on the right also gives spiritual pleasure by dancing (for a fee) at one of the city's many public shrines.

Some twenty five years ago, the government banned pedicabs from the streets
of Bangkok as a traffic hazard. Many of the drivers promptly switched to a
motorized version known as a tuk-tuk, *left, which ever since have
been contributing their own brand of chaos and also providing a popular
form of cheap transportation. A vegetable vendor, *above, gets ready
to weigh up a purchase at the Weekend Market.*

Wat Po, the largest of Bangkok's temples, was a favorite of early kings, who filled its courtyards with a highly varied assortment of exhibits aimed at educating the general public. The massive stone figures on these pages came as ballast on junks returning from the 19th-century rice trade with China; those on the right are supposedly European demons — complete with top hats.

Many aspects of Bangkok's Chinatown have changed little since the days when the district was an enclave culturally distinct from the Thai city around it. The man on the left presides over a shop filled with herbal remedies, while remnants of Chinese New Year cling to the wall above.

The cheerful girl on the left is presiding over one of the countless portable restaurants that ply Bangkok's streets, ready for business whenever a few hungry customers appear. Another familiar sight, particularly in the Chinese district, is the gold shop, above, where savings are invested in chains of varying weight; the cost of the gold is set by the government, and prices vary only with workmanship.

Among other things, Bangkok is Thailand's leading port, which means its warehouses are filled with agricultural products for shipment abroad. Rice still heads the list, as it has for centuries, but numerous other crops like maize, tapioca, and sugar are brought to the city from rural areas.

World on the Water

In 1862, by order of King Mongkut (Rama IV), construction began on a major new thoroughfare in Bangkok running for a considerable distance parallel to the Chao Phya River.

It was not the first Western-style street in the city, as some historians have claimed. King Mongkut had already built several of these, allegedly in response to complaints from foreign consuls that Western people "were accustomed for their health to take the air of an evening riding in horse-drawn carriages, and owing to the lack of suitable roads in Bangkok, they were suffering from bad health and illnesses". But New Road, as *farang* residents immediately dubbed it (the proper name was, and is, Charoen Krung), was much the longest, it boasted the city's first shophouses, and, though few realized it at the time, it signalled the beginning of the end of the original water-oriented Bangkok.

Water had conditioned Thai life from the earliest times, sustaining the vital rice fields and serving as virtually the only means of communication. The great capital of Ayutthaya, which ruled the country for 400 years, was built on an artificially-created island in the Chao Phya, and its myriad waterways serving as streets inevitably reminded European visitors of Venice.

Ayutthaya fell to the Burmese in 1767, suffering nearly total destruction, but its splendors were still very much a part of the national memory when work began on Bangkok 15 years later. Indeed, the aim of King Rama I, founder of the Chakri Dynasty which still occupies the Thai throne, was to recreate the old city as closely as possible, not only its principal buildings but also its network of *klongs* or canals. A broad *klong* was dug at a point where the river curved to form an island, which in turn was fortified with sturdy walls as Ayutthaya had been, and others followed to connect the island with the surrounding suburbs. Soon, as in Ayutthaya, they were lined with houseboats, so densely that the banks were scarcely visible, and almost the entire population went about their business by water; once again, too, accounts by *farangs* referred to "the Venice of the East".

"Thousands of shops floating in two rows are spread out before you," wrote the French Monseigneur Pallegoix, who came in the reign of Rama III, "following the curved structure of a majestic river crossed in every direction by thousands of crafts, most of which are very elegant."

None were more elegant than the fabulously carved royal barges used by the king for *kathins* or merit-making processions; of the 35 still in use the largest is some 50 meters long and requires a rowing crew of 54, brilliantly costumed and chanting in unison as they propel the fairytale creation along the river. In addition, in those early days, junks from China crowded the river along with sailing ships from far-off Europe, Arabian dhows, and ceaseless lines of huge, hump-backed sampans bringing rice, the source of Thai wealth, down from the rich Central Plains.

Crossing the Chao Phya to his home on the West bank one afternoon in 1824, an English trader noticed an equally exotic sight in the brown water. "It was," recorded a contemporary, "a creature that appeared to have two heads, four hands, and four legs, all of which were moving in perfect harmony. As Mr Hunter watched the object crawled into a nearby boat and, to his amazement, he realized that he had been looking at two small boys who were joined together at the chest".

The "object", of course, turned out to be the famous Siamese Twins (in fact they were only a quarter Siamese, the other parts being Chinese and Malay), who left their houseboat home under Hunter's auspices to find fame and fortune in the West.

Hunter also built Bangkok's first European-style brick house, an even earlier harbinger of things to come than New Road. Plenty of both imports came over the next hundred-odd years, yet water continued to play a prominent role in the city's life for a remarkably long time. When I arrived in 1960, most of the leading shops and hotels were still within a block or so of the river, and nearly every major road was bordered by *klongs*. Jim Thompson, founder of the Thai silk industry, told a reporter from the *New York Times* that he went to his office by *klong* every day; this was not really true — he only crossed one to visit the weavers behind his house — but it was not so far-fetched that the reporter disbelieved him, as he certainly would today.

I lived for ten years on Klong Saen Sap, one of the busiest, along which came a steady stream of noodle vendors in wide-brimmed straw hats, ferries with outboard engines that sounded like jets, and assorted craft carrying mountains of fruits and vegetables to the great market at Pratunam (literally, "water-gate", where there are flood locks). At night the "water babies" made their appearance. Each was in her individual boat, with discreet curtains that could be drawn and an equally discreet boatman whose job it was to keep things on an even keel and far from any nosy policemen who might be prowling on the banks. One evening there was a major crackdown a little further up the *klong* and a dozen wet water babies took refuge in my garden shrubbery until things quieted down and they could make their escape.

Has this watery world completely vanished today? A modern visitor, confronted by the demands of 900,000 registered motor vehicles (add another 100,000 by the time you read this) might think so. New Road is passé, the smart shops gone to other areas, and a view of the Chao Phya is as exotic to the average city resident as it is to a guest at the venerable old Oriental Hotel.

The pungent *klong* I briefly overlooked from my very first house is now part of a six-lane, perpetually-jammed avenue; where the house was there is now a massage parlor, aptly named the Sahara.

But Bangkok is not really as arid as all that. (In the rainy season, it is not arid at all: numerous roads revert to the *klongs* they replaced, and a bird's eye view would give a fairly good idea of where the old waterways coursed). The *klong* that Jim Thompson crossed daily still flows past his famous Thai house; in fact, it flows better than in his time, thanks to belated recognition of the role it plays in flood drainage and a consequent large-scale dredging operation. The water babies, so I am told, are gone; but Klong Saen Sap is still an important communications route, and if you take a boat up from Pratunam you will find the scenery little changed from what I knew. And the great river, though no longer the focal point it was, still offers a busy panorama of rice barges, ships calling at the Port of Bangkok, and smaller vessels of all kinds.

Perhaps the best evidence of continuity lies in Dhonburi, across the river, now a part of the metropolitan area. Dhonburi, too, has acquired roads and rowshops, but its many old *klongs* remain integral to its life, winding past market gardens, lush orchards of durian and mango, temples that flash like improbable fantasies in the sunlight, and teeming communities of open-fronted houses on the water, each a little stage-set for human drama.

Gliding down almost any of these waterways, a visitor can be at once transported into the past and also reminded that it is still very much a part of the present.

A vast variety of merchandise moves along the klongs *of Bangkok and Dhonburi, sometimes supplying waterside residents, sometimes supplying one of the many markets. A floating noodle vendor, left, is usually around to supply freshly-cooked food, while basket loads of vegetables come into the city from the surrounding suburbs.*

In old Bangkok the klongs *served as streets, and they still do in certain parts of Dhonburi. Above, a monk receives his morning meal from a house on the waterway, having travelled by boat from his nearby temple. The father and son on the right view the passing scene from their boat, the eyes on which are supposed to ward off evil spirits.*

The scenery along the banks of the Chao Phya River has changed less than almost any other aspect of Bangkok. Dozens of wats raise their distinctive soaring rooftops behind rows of simple river-side houses, while here and there can be glimpsed reminders of 19th-century missionary effort like the recently-restored Holy Rosary Church on the left.

Overleaf, a typical Chao Phya panorama. Ferry boats ply constantly between the two banks, mostly carrying Dhonburi-based commuters back and forth to work in the city, and endless processions of sampans, riding low in the water, bring rice from the fertile Central Plains on which the capital has traditionally depended for sustenance.

*Though sometimes murky-looking to an outsider's eye, the river and klongs
of Bangkok yield a steady supply of edible fish, like those on the left
set out to dry in the sun. The couple above operate a boat selling charcoal,
still a basic cooking fuel in many Thai kitchens.*

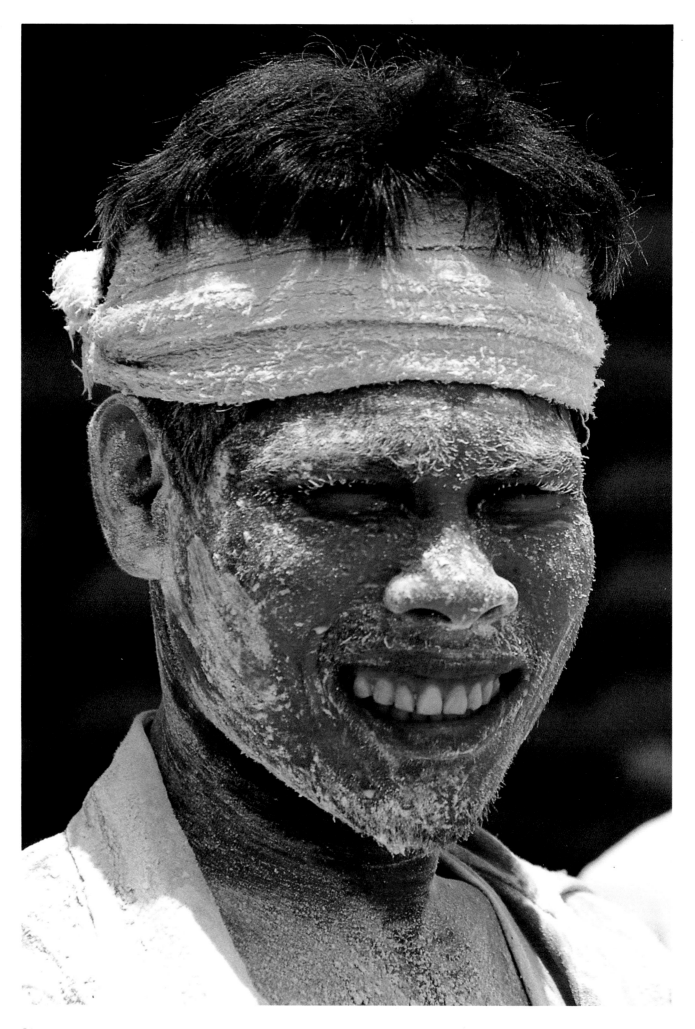

A ship at Klong Toey, the Port of Bangkok, is loaded by laborers, most of whom have migrated to the capital from provincial villages in search of a better life. More often than not they have ended up in one of the extensive slums that have grown up around the port.

Overleaf, the contrasts that add so much to Bangkok's appeal are nowhere more evident than along the broad Chao Phya River. Luxury hotels and office blocks form a skyline that overlooks rice-laden sampans, ferries, tug-boats, and assorted other craft that have changed little in the past century.

*Despite the beauty of their intricate workmanship, the floral arrangements that
adorn the boats on these pages are not placed there for mere decoration.
Refreshed daily by the drivers, with a prayer or two, they are propitiary offerings to
ensure a profitable day of ferrying passengers along the* klongs *and river
by pleasing whatever spirits might be around.*

On land or water, the Thais are inveterate snackers, a tendency
catered to by innumerable food vendors of all kinds. The girl with the
floating kitchen on the left — wearing an ingenious traditional hat that both
wards off the sun and allows air to circulate below — can whip up
a nutritious meal in a matter of minutes. Above, a lone boat
heads for home along the river at day's end.

*After years of moving eastward into former suburban rice fields, Bangkok seems
to be gradually returning to the great river that dominated its early days.
The high-priced new condominium on the left is one of several signs of this recent
development. This one is located on the Dhonburi side and, besides spectacular views
of riverine life, owners get a free ferryboat service to ease problems of commuting.*

A Spiritual Spectrum

For sheer razzle-dazzle splendor, few creations of man can equal a Thai *wat* — or Buddhist temple complex — of which there are some 300 in Bangkok and far more if you include Dhonburi across the river. Their spires and swooping roofs rise like rare jewels out of the muddy sea of contemporary architecture, offering both a highly visible link to the city's early days, when rulers competed for the honor of building new ones, and also ample testimony to the faith still followed by the overwhelming majority of Thais.

The power of Buddhism is most apparent at the village level, where the *wat* is a central feature of secular as well as spiritual life. In Bangkok, on the other hand, the more celebrated temples often seem to exist in curious isolation, glittering stage sets that have little apparent relationship to the city around them. Except on one of the big Buddhist festival days, tourists are likely to see more of their own kind than Thais; even at ordinary *wats,* attendance at the regular prayers and sermons is often sparse and mainly composed of older people. From a Thai experience limited to Bangkok it would be easy to conclude that Buddhism no longer exerts the sort of force that produced these magnificent monuments, particularly among the predominant young.

Such an impression would be wrong. For all its big-city bustle, Bangkok is essentially a place of transplanted villagers; and while distance, distractions, and lack of community spirit may conspire to keep them from using the temple as freely as they would back home, the philosophy it represents is manifested in countless ways.

Among the most evident is the Buddhist concept of making merit and thereby improving the quality of future existences. This concept lay behind the building of the *wats* and their frequent restoration over the years; it also motivates the common practice of offering food to monks, usually not on a regular basis but to mark some special occasion like a birthday. Merit is also gained by releasing captive birds, fish, and turtles, by giving to beggars, by organizing festive groups to carry various offerings of a practical nature (robes, soap, toilet paper, etc.) to a needy temple, sometimes in the city but more often in some distant province.

Nearly every Bangkok home contains at least one Buddha image somewhere in a place of honor, often dozens of them in a special

"Buddha room", and prayers are offered daily by members of the family. Most Thai males, moreover, whether city or country-bred, will enter the monkhood at some point in their lives, usually just before they are ready to get married and settle down. And monks are invariably called on to chant prayers for the dead, prior to cremation, in rites that can last anywhere from a few nights to a full year in the case of high royalty.

But Buddhism is not the only spiritual presence at large in Thailand. Older, deeply-entrenched beliefs in spirits, astrology, amulets, and other supernatural forces also command widespread allegiance; and the pragmatic, tolerant Thais see no conflict in boldly mixing them all together in a blend as subtle as the hot, sweet, and sour flavors of their food.

In just about every compound, for instance, commercial as well as residential, one finds a graceful little structure atop a pole: a miniature wooden Thai house in some cases, in others an imposing replica of a Buddhist temple, brightly colored and ornately decorated. This is the home of the compound's powerful guardian spirit, who must be regularly placated with offerings of fresh flowers, joss sticks, occasionally food, if the human occupants are to enjoy peace and prosperity. When things go wrong it is often necessary to call in a spiritual expert — who may well turn out to be a Buddhist monk, to the confusion of outsiders who like their categories kept neatly separate.

Cities, too, have guardian spirits. Bangkok's resides at Lak Muang, the "city pillar", established by King Rama I just across from the Grand Palace at a site that marked the exact geographical center of his original capital. People come to it by the thousands to ask for better jobs, relief from illness, romantic success, a winning number in the national lottery, pledging in return assorted offerings or performances of Thai classical dance.

Bangkok also has countless other shrines serving various needs. There is one at every hospital, for obvious reasons, and at every district police station. Tucked away behind the Hilton Hotel is one inhabited by a female spirit whose offerings consist mostly of phalluses, some highly realistic and of immense size. I got to know this shrine very well since I lived next door to it for a number of years, and as far as I could observe the majority of supplicants came with quite routine requests; this did not prevent some *farang* residents from conjuring up all sorts of fevered legends, however, several of which later turned up in the celebrated *Emmanuelle*.

Probably the most popular shrine in the city is located in the compound of the government-owned Erawan Hotel, and is dedicated to the Hindu god Brahma. Originally erected to stop a series of mishaps during construction of the hotel, the shrine proved equally effective with problems brought by the general public; so that today, considerably expanded, it is nearly always jammed with believers. (The spirit is supposed to be partial to pretty girls, which explains a collection of dancers regularly on hand for paid performances when wishes are granted. There is a story that one eminently respectable lady promised to dance naked if her urgent request was met; it was and she did, supposedly in the small hours of the morning when no one was about).

Astrology plays a prominent role in Thai life, determining auspicious dates for getting married, opening a business, taking trips, and countless other activities. Fortune tellers, too, are frequently consulted, as well as mediums who often go into quite dramatic trances when they communicate with the spirit world (one old man I saw assumed the voice and mannerisms of a flirtatious young girl).

Around the neck of nearly every Thai male, and that of many females too, hangs some sort of amulet, often in the form of a Buddhist votive tablet; at least six regular publications are devoted exclusively to such charms, with expert advice on how to tell the real from the bogus and testimonials from owners who have survived horrific experiences.

In times of dire emergency, Thais will call on all the spiritual resources at their disposal. There was a wealthy woman, for example, who in a careless moment swallowed a packet of needles. Her doctor recommended an emergency operation but the lady, having dread of surgery, insisted on three days to try other methods. She prayed first to the powerful Emerald Buddha, offering 500 boiled eggs if he interceded; then she went to the Erawan Shrine, where she pledged a performance by the prettiest of the dancing girls; finally she bought a small but powerful magnet which she placed in a strategic spot while she slept.

Whether through Buddhism, Brahma, or natural science, the needles made a harmless appearance on the third day. All the promises were kept by the grateful lady, who gave the magnet to a nephew; he now carries it as an amulet.

The power of a Buddha image, to the devout, lies in its ability to induce a mood of serenity, and Bangkok's temples contain thousands like those at Wat Po on the left. A novice, above, goes through one of the final ceremonies before being ordained, a rite of passage undertaken by nearly every Thai man at some period in his life.

Walking three times around the main building of a temple complex carrying joss sticks, lotus buds, and other offerings, preceding pages, is one of the rituals performed on major Buddhist holidays throughout Thailand.
The procession here is taking place at Wat Benchamabopitr, usually called the Marble Temple, built in the early years of the present century and the last of Bangkok's royally-sponsored monasteries.

Presenting food to Buddhist monks is one of the most fundamental ways of earning merit. City-dwellers sometimes do it at mass ceremonies to observe a special occasion, like those above outside the Marble Temple. At left, monks stroll through a temple courtyard — a scene that changes little over the passing years.

Apart from serving as centers for sermons and religious contemplation, Buddhist temples also play an important role in community life. Almost every young Thai male enters the priesthood at some time, usually just before he gets married and embarks on a career; but many, particularly those from poor families, become novices as children and receive their secular education within the temple precincts.

Somerset Maugham found Bangkok's temples "gorgeous ... defying the
brilliancy of nature and supplementing it with the ingenuity and playful
boldness of man". Splendor of decoration is an important component of Thai
Buddhist art, as seen in the mosaic-covered guardians from classical
mythology on the left and in Buddha images kept constantly
gleaming with fresh applications of gold leaf, above.

Overleaf, fantasy achieves an ultimate peak in the dazzling sprawl of
Wat Phra Keo, which forms part of the compound containing the Grand Palace.
Here resides the famous Emerald Buddha, protector of the entire nation,
surrounded by a literally breathtaking mélange of temple buildings, pavilions,
golden chedis, and mythological statuary, regularly added to and refurbished
by all the kings of the present Chakri Dynasty.

The small but powerful Emerald Buddha, left, (actually carved from semi-precious nephrite) sits dressed in its cool season robes of solid gold filigree. Above is a portion of the huge, 46-meter Reclining Buddha at Wat Po.

An appearance of effortless grace is an ideal sought by every Thai Buddhist
monk, whether walking on a public street with his alms bowl or alone
in a temple cloister. Movements that invite awkwardness —
running, for instance, or riding a bicycle — are avoided, especially
when laymen are present.

The colossal standing Buddha at Wat Intrawiharn attracts numerous worshipers who come to pray at its massive golden feet and, as often as not, to ask for assistance in a wide variety of personal problems. Offerings usually consist of scented floral wreaths, joss sticks and, occasionally, bowls of food.

The unusual shrine on these pages, which stands now in the garden of the Hilton Hotel, is not restricted to supplicants with fertility problems, as many foreign visitors deduce from its favored offerings. The lingam *also represents prosperity in general, and those who seek favors from the resident female spirit (whose name is Tuptim) are as likely to ask for luck in the lottery drawing as for the birth of a child.*

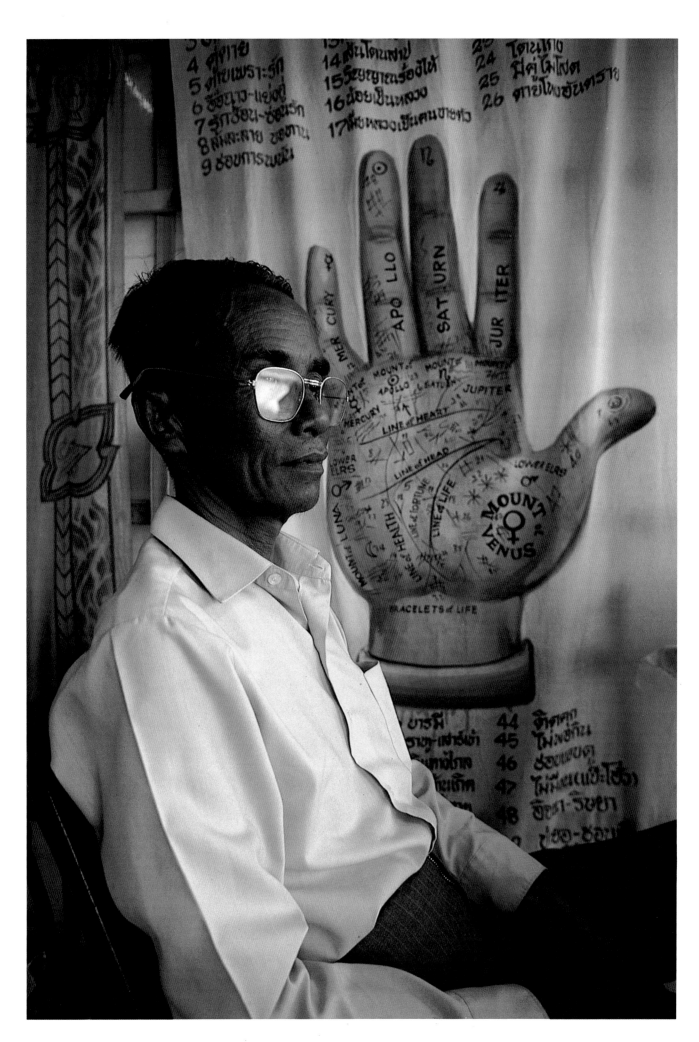

Buddhism is the professed religion of the vast majority of Thais, but assorted
beliefs in the occult also figure prominently in the lives of most people.
Astrologers, for example, are consulted prior to important undertakings, such as
opening a new business or choosing an auspicious marriage date,
and fortune tellers of all kinds are routinely called on for glimpses of the future.

A visitor wandering around the Yawaraj District, Bangkok's Chinatown, will see many Chinese temples, like the one left, and traditional decorations. Overleaf, incense is lit to pay respects to Chinese ancestors.

Beauty Sacred and Profane

Whenever I have to pass through Bangkok's Chinatown, on my way to one of the government offices on the other side of the city, I always watch for a certain bridge over a narrow *klong.* It is easy to miss in that confused neighborhood, but if I am lucky — especially if I get caught in a traffic jam on the bridge itself — I am rewarded with a sight that never fails to stir me.

The *klong* is actually not much more than an oily, pungent stream, the buildings along it merely ordinary rowshops, their once gaudy colors faded to pastels by years of rain and sun. As seen from the bridge, though, especially in the kindly light of early morning or late afternoon, the view of the slightly curving waterway and the rippling reflections of ocher and burnt sienna has a magical quality that I find not only intensely romantic but also truly beautiful.

Several decades of reckless and mostly unimaginative construction (often accompanied by equally reckless destruction), the insatiable demands of the automobile, the natural nervous energy of a relatively young city determined to modernize at all costs: these have produced the greater part of contemporary Bangkok and to most visitors the result is not very pleasing from an aesthetic standpoint. Yet along with its many other surprises, the city does contain a remarkable amount of beauty — sometimes hidden from public view, sometimes accidental like my view from the bridge, sometimes justly celebrated.

Pre-eminent in the latter category· are the surviving monuments of Bangkok's early years, when Thai arts enjoyed a brief but remarkable renaissance. All the first three Chakri kings shared a dream of recreating the splendor of lost Ayutthaya, and all were enthusiastic builders and restorers; King Rama III, for example, built nine new temples during his 27-year reign and made extensive repairs and additions to more than 60 others. To assist them they had a small army of the country's finest craftsmen, some of whom had worked in Ayutthaya itself: superb carpenters and woodcarvers, anonymous painters of vast murals, artisans skilled at delicate mosaic work, mother-of-pearl inlay, gold-and-black lacquer painting, the casting of richly-robed Buddha images.

Their work adorns nearly all the *wats* in the older part of the city, as well as many in Dhonburi on the other side of the river, where some of the finest temple murals are to be seen. Undoubtedly the greatest concentration, though, is crowded into the mile-square compound that contains the Grand Palace and its adjacent royal temple, home to the first five kings and also to the sacred Emerald Buddha, a small green image of northern Thai origin which Rama I rescued from a long exile in Laos.

A stroll through the temple precincts is a psychedelic experience. Scarcely an inch seems to have been left untouched by brilliant mosaics, intricate carving, lavish coatings of gold leaf, bold color combinations; elegant buildings and pavilions rise everywhere you look, multi-tiered roofs straining towards the sky, and mythological creatures both fierce and quaint gaze down from every stairway. It sounds too much, and perhaps for some refined tastes it may be. For others, though — among them myself — the whole dazzling mass achieves a strange and wonderful harmony that lingers in the memory with the resonance of true art.

The last royal temple to be built in Bangkok was Wat Benchamabopitr, popularly called the Marble Temple, completed in 1901 by Rama V. Westernization was in full swing at the time, and many of the traditional arts were in danger; the Marble Temple was a successful fusion of the two, seldom, alas, to be attempted again and never to be done so well. To me one of the most beautiful Bangkok sights is the colonnaded courtyard lit by the last rays of a sunset, the serene gray Italian marble contrasting with the muted gold of the rooftiles and the almost shockingly vivid saffron robes of monks filing into the central building for evening prayers.

There is beauty, too, in many of the old European-style buildings that have managed so far to escape the grim fate of "development". Along the river, for instance, there are the splendid, cream-colored offices of the East Asiatic Company (whose founder also built the nearby Oriental Hotel), the stately French Embassy with its lawn running down to the bank, a rather dilapidated but still imposing building that used to be the Customs House (now a river fire station), and numerous Victorian palaces in various stages of disrepair. One of my own favorites, elsewhere in the city, is the former Phya Thai Palace which has seen service as a royal residence, as a luxury hotel, and, for the past 50 years, as a military hospital. Aesthetics is hardly uppermost in the minds of its present occupants, but the old buildings manage somehow to display a remarkable degree of their original elegance, extending even to a neglected little Greek pavilion in what remains of the once-extensive garden. A 1929 guidebook, written during the palace's hotel period, says that performances of the Thai classical dance were given in the pavilion on full-moon nights, and I often think how lovely those gorgeous bejewelled costumes must have looked against the Attic simplicity of the white columns.

Beauty of a less exalted sort can be found by the discerning eye all over the city. Plunge, for instance, into any public market, ignore the din and smells, and observe the consummate artistry with which most of the foods are displayed to attract shoppers: dried fish turning graceful cartwheels, oranges in precise pyramids, bamboo trays of mangoes shading delicately from green to gold, bananas arranged to resemble the unfolding petals of a huge flower.

Or look at the floral wreaths offered in such lavish abundance at any shrines hung for good luck on taxi-cab mirrors, presented in welcome to honored guests: even the simplest is a small work of art, highly perishable to be sure but nonetheless painstakingly constructed in patterns traditional for centuries.

I remember once being taken on a rare private tour of the old "inside" section of the Grand Palace, formerly an all-female domain into which only the king could come without special permission. It was a haunted, half-forgotten world of shuttered villas, empty streets, and overgrown gardens, but it was not deserted: in the shade of an ancient tamarind tree sat a group of elderly women, weaving the most beautiful jasmine wreaths I had ever seen. They wove more than a hundred a day, I was told, exclusively for the use of the present royal family in their many ceremonial activities, just as others in the same place did when Bangkok was young.

And at least some people find a bizarre beauty in one of the commonest city sights: the immense movie posters that dominate many intersections with lurid depictions of sex, violence, and other cinematic pleasures. The average Bangkok resident scarcely notices these handpainted extravaganzas. Not so the sophisticated French: some years ago, 20 original posters and 200 reproductions went for a month-long exhibition at the respectable Musée d'Art Moderne de la Ville de Paris, where thousands of art-lovers were treated to such sights as Krasue Sao, a legendary ghost from North-eastern Thailand, always shown as a disembodied head trailing a long mass of realistically rendered intestines.

The monumental chedi *of Wat Arun, the Temple of Dawn, is one of
Bangkok's landmarks, its central tower rising 86 meters on the bank of the
Chao Phya. The entire structure is covered with millions of bits of
ceramic and porcelain to form an almost unbroken pattern. From one of
its upper terraces, above, a visitor has a breathtaking view of the curving
river and the spires of the Grand Palace.*

*Overleaf, bold splashes of color are an integral part of Thai ceremonies,
especially those involving royalty. These splendidly uniformed young men are
participants in a parade that accompanied the lavish cremation of a former
Queen, their outfits faithfully copied from those worn in
similar rituals during the 19th century.*

Thailand's National Museum, above, and the nearby Temple of the Reclining Buddha, left, were built in the early years of Bangkok when the classic Thai arts enjoyed a major revival. Doors, windows, walls, columns and ceilings are all covered with some of the finest surviving examples of mural painting, mother-of-pearl inlay and gold-and-black lacquerwork.

Overleaf, traditional Thai painting is two-dimensional and highly decorative, often with gold leaf applied. The scenes are usually religious — telling the life of the Buddha or the moralistic Jataka tales — but sometimes, as in this example, they present excerpts from classical mythology.

The boys and girls at left and above are students at the Dramatic Art College, formed by the Fine Arts Department to maintain the long tradition of training youngsters in the Thai classical dance. Whether or not they ever actually perform on a stage, the rigorous exercises will help develop the supple grace of movement much admired by Thais in ordinary life.

The huge stone figure, left, came from China in the early 19th century while Thai mythology inspired the fearsome image above. Overleaf, Wat Arun's 86-meter landmark tower symbolizing Mount Meru holding up the world.

The first Bangkok king dreamed of recreating the splendors of the lost Ayutthaya, destroyed in 1767, and artisans flocked to the new capital to help him realize it. Among their creations were incredible jewel-like mosaics.

The use of slender gold ornaments to elongate the fingertips originated in
northern Thailand, but it is now a standard feature in traditional dance
performances all over the country. The art of hand-painted parasols of cloth
or paper also comes from the north and turns up in most Bangkok handicraft shops.

An innate elegance of line distinguishes many of the objects used in ordinary Thai
life, as revealed in the hand-made umbrella, left, that shelters a market vendor.
Newly-minted, plastic-shrouded Buddha images, above, await enshrinement
in one of the numerous temples in and around Bangkok, probably thanks to a
wealthy donor who will, in turn, gain merit for his pious act.

What appears at first glance to be huge nosegays, left, on sale at a Bangkok flower
market are in fact bunches of lotus buds, widely used as offerings in Buddhist
temples and shrines. Elsewhere, water lily fanciers can select a specimen or two
from displays, like the one above, to plant in ponds or water jars at home.

Classical Thai dance was once staged only at the royal court. Then as now the dancers wore costumes that echoed the city's architectural splendor and relied on a lengthy vocabulary of gesture and posture to tell epic stories of love and war.

Colorful patterns run like bright threads through the texture of daily Thai existence. Left, monks arrange a vase of roses (locally-grown, by the way) for use on their temple's altars. A walk through any market reveals many more mundane forms of patterned beauty.

Artisans applied lavish decorations to almost every inch of both palaces
and temples. The airy pavilion, above, now in the compound of the
National Museum, was formerly part of the palace of the Deputy King.
The buildings on the right, of ceramic tiles, are Wat Rajabopit,
built in 1863 by King Chulalongkorn.

Overleaf, Hollywood at its most imaginative would find it hard to duplicate the
mind-boggling reality of Wat Phra Keo, the Temple of the Emerald Buddha.
Gaudily dressed figures from Thai legend support a vast golden chedi,
carved roof-ends strain like graceful fingers toward the sky, and mosaic-covered
towers rise, all surveyed by half-human, half-animal creatures that might
have been dreamed up by Walt Disney in one of his more whimsical moments.

Sanuk Diversions

Anyone who spends much time in Thailand, whether in Bangkok or in the smallest village, will soon become familiar with the term *sanuk,* usually translated as "fun" or "pleasure", though these scarcely do justice to its range. A substantial part of Thai life, in fact, can be divided into the two broad categories of things that are *sanuk* and things that aren't, the latter being just about the worst possible criticism of any undertaking.

Sanuk is not limited to the obvious, like games and parties; almost any activity can earn the accolade under the right circumstances. Hard work can be *sanuk* providing it is not routine or solitary (nothing done everyday is *sanuk,* and neither is anything done alone); so can a certain class, shopping in a particular market, even an apparently solemn ceremony.

Why some experiences fail to qualify is harder for an outsider to say, but the evaluation is instinctive and merciless. A Thai woman I knew went to Russia on a cultural tour, and when she returned I asked her what she thought of it. "Not *sanuk,*" she pronounced, with grim finality, as a judge might condemn a mass murderer; and with that, Russia was finished.

Bangkok is undoubtedly the greatest national resource of *sanuk* of all kinds, for rich and poor alike. Without spending more than a few *baht* for bus fare, not even that if his legs are strong, a wide-eyed newcomer from the provinces can find enough opportunities to keep him happily diverted for weeks; the better-heeled are confronted with an array to last a lifetime.

Festivals and fairs are by definition *sanuk* and the Bangkok year is liberally sprinkled with both. Two New Years are observed, the Western one at the end of December and the old Thai one in mid-April, both with all-out celebrations; Chinese New Year is not an official holiday, though it might as well be since most of the city shuts down. On the King's birthday, the whole city is decorated and the oval field across from the Grand Palace is turned into a vast fair with musical shows and as many as 100 outdoor movies being shown simultaneously. At Loy Krathong, the prettiest of festivals, thousands of little candle-lit boats shaped like lotuses are set adrift in every pond and water-way as votive offerings. Meanwhile loud-speakers play folk songs at top volume. (*Sanuk,* it might be noted, is rarely associated with introspective serenity and quiet).

Public markets in general are *sanuk,* especially the huge Weekend Market, formerly held against the peerless backdrop of the Emerald Buddha Temple but now removed to Chatuchak Park in the suburbs. The new setting is certainly less spectacular, but the market remains as wonderfully varied as ever, with a range of goods that extends from frying pans and fresh fruits to baby pythons and pre-historic beads. Popular with the young — and more than half of Bangkok's population is under 30 — are the new shopping centers that have mushroomed throughout the city in such extraordinary profusion. Relatively few of them go as customers; it is simply *sanuk* to stroll for hours about the air-conditioned corridors, looking at the window displays of far-out clothes, listening to the disco music that emanates from most shops, perhaps striking up a bit of romance.

All sports are *sanuk,* whether participated in or merely watched. In the relative cool of late afternoon, every park, vacant lot, or construction site has its groups of young men playing soccer, volleyball, or *takraw,* the latter a game of almost balletic grace in which a rattan ball is passed from player to player using every part of the body except the hands. The national favorite is boxing, both the familiar Western style and the far freer Thai variety in which the feet are transformed into lethal weapons; whenever a world championship match is televised, Bangkok's streets are eerily empty and every coffee shop is jammed with cheering fans.

Gambling is officially frowned upon — the newspapers regularly carry pictures of sheepish-looking middle-aged women who have been caught red-handed at a game of cards or mah-jongg — but so high does it rank on the *sanuk* scale that all efforts to stamp it out are probably doomed. Boxing matches, football games, horse races, and all the usual competitions inspire wagers; and so do more esoteric ones like kite fights and combat between pairs of gorgeously-hued male Siamese fighting fish. At times, a distinct note of desperation seems to creep into the search for something *sanuk* to bet on: not long ago, passing a group of excited boys huddled over a stream created by a broken water pipe, I discovered they were placing one-*baht* bets on a race between two bottle-caps.

When evening falls, the *sanuk* horizon broadens considerably. Thais love going out to eat, especially in groups, and Bangkok has thousands of places to satisfy the whim, ranging from huge garden establishments with live entertainment to five or six tables blocking a public sidewalk (no pedestrian would dream of complaining). There are reasonably respectable nightclubs where a man could take his wife (but usually doesn't) and discos plain and fancy (ear-splitting in either case) for the young. Bowling, once a popular pastime, has waned; but roller discos are very much in, occasioning a good deal of head-shaking among older, traditional Thais.

More purely male-oriented pleasures abound, to such an extent that Bangkok has acquired a dubious international reputation and attracts jet-loads of eager tourists from less tolerant lands. Most of them head straight for Patpong, once a single street with one or two staid piano bars but now a whole network of alleyways chock-a-block with raucous establishments catering to just about any taste. ("You want a dwarf?" a pimp whispered to me once).

It is a world of gaudy neon, of whimsical names (The Horny Toad has closed, but Madness is still going strong and so is a gay place called The Lonely Boy), of non-stop music that manages to drown out even the noise of the traffic, of gyrating girls in G-strings, of sidewalk beauties whose gender is debatable, of "special shows" that involve extraordinary physical skills.

Then there are the celebrated massage parlors, equally esteemed by both Thai men and visitors. Myth proclaims these materialized during the era of the Vietnam War and R & R; in fact, there were quite a few when I first came to Bangkok, long before the GI's made their appearance on the scene. Undeniably, though, they have increased in size, splendor, and amenities over the past two decades, and many today have achieved a high level of fantasy with sunken baths, one-way mirrors, Niagara-like waterfalls, and services with mysterious names like "sandwich" and "because".

Sanuk need not end when the discos close and the last drop of soapy water disappears down the drain. This is the busiest time for the city's innumerable "short-time" motels, many so constructed that a car can drive right up to the door of the room while a curtain immediately drops to hide the license plate from prying eyes.

On my first visit to Bangkok, I innocently checked into one of these establishments for three weeks, to the bemusement of the managers. I wasn't innocent for long of course — about three hours, to be precise — but I stayed the full term, learned a lot about round-the-clock *sanuk* (afternoons are busy, too), and gained a certain celebrity as the first guest in history ever to receive mail.

Anyone can master the intricacies of the Thai classical dance, at least in a snapshot, like the one left, to send the folks back home. Above, the shadow play, with painted figures made of leather, probably came to Thailand from Indonesia; once a feature of every festival, it is comparatively rare nowadays.

Sanuk *pleasures — for the girl, left, it's playing* saw duang, *a traditional Thai two-stringed fiddle, and for the venerable member of Bangkok's sizeable Indian community it's an evening stroll in the park.*

Sanuk *fads are fickle, sometimes lasting only for a season or two. One that seems to be here to stay is skating — both roller and ice — and a Bangkok shopping center has an ice-skating rink which is attracting crowds of adventurous younger residents, eager to escape the heat for a few hours and demonstrate their skills to the beat of ear-splitting disco music.*

Thai boxing is an irresistible blend of ritual, balletic grace, and savage assault with just about every part of the body being employed: the real attraction for most fans is the footwork of their traditional fighters.

Surprises abound on Bangkok streets, among them the two vendors above
demonstrating the effectiveness of their wares. The boys on the right are
making a selection from the wide variety of hand-made kites on sale at
Sanam Luang, the broad field near the Emerald Buddha Temple.
In the hot season, late-afternoon breezes sweep the field
and make it a popular haunt for kite flyers of all ages.

Overleaf, a stall displays several local liquors, among them Chinese brandy
and Thai whisky. The latter is a prominent feature of nearly every
sanuk get-together of Thai men and is usually drunk with soda and a
squeeze of lime juice; not as strong as foreign whiskies but
sufficiently so to enliven an evening.

Snakes may not be everybody's bag, but the young lady above seems to be enjoying the two pythons available for picture taking at an amusement park just outside Bangkok. The motorcyclist on the left, however, is clearly taken aback by the creature he has just encountered on a city street.

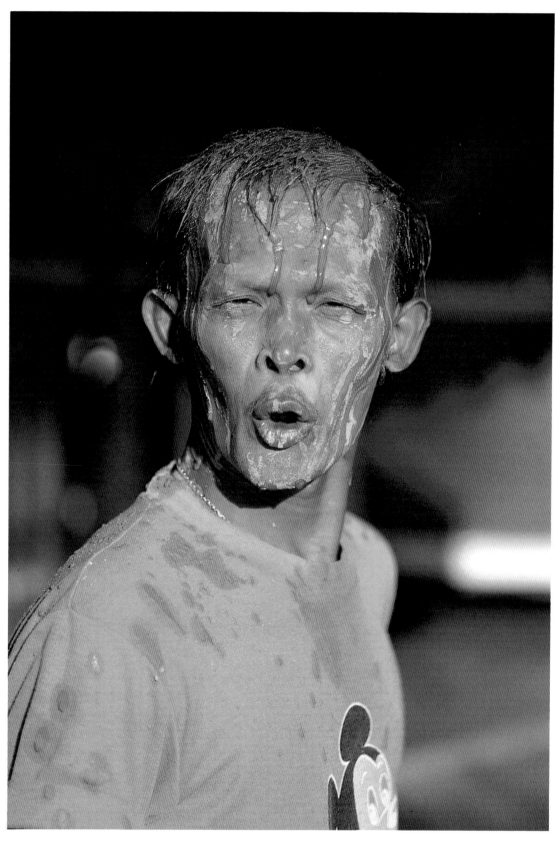

For all the inroads made by television, Thai movies still attract large audiences.
Comedians like the one above are often kept busy working on five or six
films at the same time. And gigantic movie posters adorn every Bangkok theater.

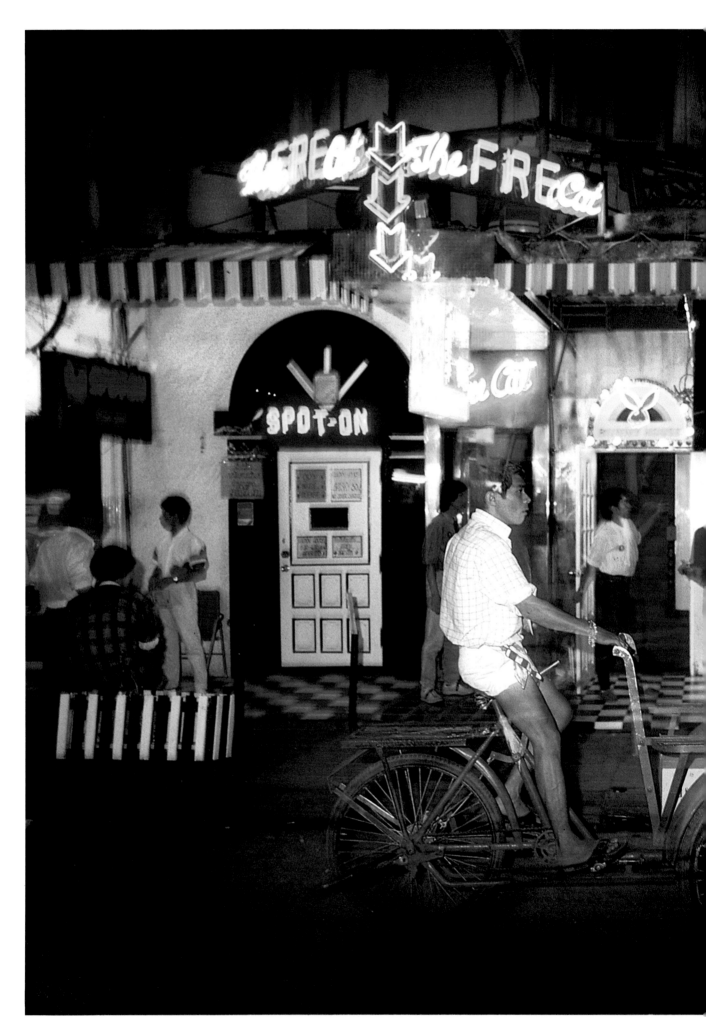

151

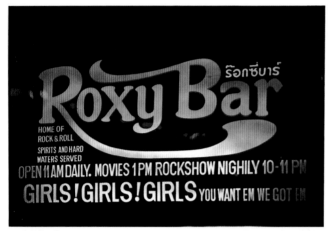

Patpong – once a single street but now a whole area – is Bangkok's most celebrated nightlife center. Bars and discos open and close with rather bewildering speed, but just about anything except peace and quiet is available for a price once the sun goes down.

Previous pages, the Patpong scene is a memorable mixture of bustle, sleaze, and gaudy neon, with the raucous throb of disco music never far away. Touts outside every bar offer a wide variety of enticements to lure the evening crowds into their own particular establishment.

GIRLS, GIRLS, GIRLS promises more than one Patpong bar, and bevies of scantily-clad beauties are indeed the principal attraction for most of the night-time trade. Thanks to migration from poor provincial villages, the supply appears to be inexhaustible, to the dismay of many social workers and the delight of visitors from less tolerant lands.

Overleaf, the fame of Bangkok's lavish, multi-storey massage parlors now stretches to remote parts of the world. In many, the girls sit demurely behind one-way glass so that a client can discreetly make his selection.

Eternal Bangkok

In 1928 a special committee which had been appointed to study possible town planning in Bangkok submitted its preliminary report to King Prajadhipok, Thailand's last absolute ruler. On close examination the king found it wanting, and for a fairly basic reason: town planning, he pointed out, requires a certain idea of the future and "things are still changing very rapidly, so that we cannot make predictions even ten years ahead".

Despite all the soothsayers at their disposal, most people who live in the city would probably agree that the future is no clearer today. Former residents who have been away only a few years return to find whole neighborhoods gone or altered almost beyond recognition, once-quiet lanes transformed into six-lane speedways, more and more rowshops and housing estates creeping eastward across a low lying expanse once known as "The Sea of Mud", which had played a part in the original siting of Bangkok since Rama I expected it to deter would-be invaders approaching from that direction. (Nowadays this is the area that suffers the worst floods, a fact that ought not to surprise anyone but does).

As it turned out, no enemy ever attempted to cross The Sea of Mud. Nor did the dream of recreating the legendary Ayutthaya progress very far once the city began to display its own peculiar dynamics. Nor, perhaps more significantly, did anything much come of a later plan by Rama V to turn Bangkok into a European–style capital of broad, fashionable boulevards and public gardens. Maugham saw some of these efforts on his first visit and found them "handsome, spacious, and stately, shaded by trees, the deliberate adornment of a great city devised by a king ambitious to have an imposing seat; but they have no reality ... No one walks in them".

Instead, people were walking in the crowded alleyways of Chinatown and along then-smart New Road. Later they would be walking down busy streets in areas Rama V would have regarded as inconceivably remote countryside.

Unpredictability, then, has always been one of the chief characteristics of Bangkok's growth, and is likely to remain so. It is just as much a part of its everyday life: frustrating to those who thrive on the familiar and like to know what lies ahead, infinitely exciting to those who relish the prospect of discovery and adventure.

The photographer would like to thank
Patrick Gauvain and Alexander Bowie
for their guidance in Patpong.

First printed: March 1986
Publisher's number: 287